I am a Strong Woman
these are my stories

a guided journal

I am a Strong Woman
these are my stories

The Strong Woman who owns this Journal and these stories is:

_____

(contact)

and she's proud of it!

Hello, Friend.

I have been very fortunate in my life for so many reasons. One of them is that I have a family who loves to tell stories. At birthday or holiday gatherings, the conversation will quickly turn to, "remember when" or "when I was about your age" stories. Those, in turn, result in deep, soul cleansing laughter. Even on our saddest days, we share stories. The importance of this legacy was really brought home to me when my mother died. In her last few days, she continued to tell me of times in her life and although I thought we'd talked about every possible thing, I had so many more questions when she died. Remembering her stories gave me strength and comfort just as telling them did for her.

The truth is we all have stories – no matter our age, generation, or any other demographic we fall into. We are each unique. Each wonderfully made. And we've all made choices.

Sometimes we want our stories told but we just can't speak them or, unfortunately, we think no one is listening.

But our stories make us who we are.

This book is in honor of my mother and it comes with a request. Understand that your stories matter. They need to be told. They teach. They inspire. They thrill. They entertain. They show the people in your life how deeply you loved and how deeply you are loved. So my request is, tell your stories

This book is not intended to be used as a workbook. Don't feel compelled to go in the order the prompts are written. Don't even feel compelled to use the prompts that are included. If you don't want to answer a particular question, mark it out and add your own. Write in the margins, in crayon, upside down. This is a place to tell your stories IN YOUR WAY. The questions included here are just the starting point. How your stories are told, and which stories you tell, are completely yours.

 I also hope that on those days when you may not feel strong, when life seems to hit you full on, you can go back and read what you've written. There will be strength here. And love. And dreams. Let them remind you of who you really are: an incredibly strong woman.

A strong woman inspired this book.

Another strong woman will fill its pages.

Blessings and Peace Always,

Jennifer

The most adventurous thing I've ever done is. . . .

The first time I fell in love was. . .

My favorite game when I was a child...

The best

book I

ever

read. . .

My
Favorite
birthday
was...

The clothes that make me feel most confident are...

If I could
live my

perfect day

I would...

How I
met my best
friend...

How I would describe my faith...

The song

I always

sing along

with is...

My

favorite

meal is....

I cry
when
I think
about...

The hardest thing I've forgiven...

The best

advice I

ever

received...

How I learned to drive...

I would like to learn how to...

The job I
liked

best was....

I would describe my family as...

When I was in high school, I loved to…

My
proudest
moment
was...

My

favorite

flower

is...

If I
could go
anywhere in
the world it
would be...

Holidays

make me

feel...

This makes me
laugh
every time....

My

favorite

season

is...

I like

to be

alone

when...

One habit
I'd like
to start is....

Someone
I'd like
to thank is...

I wish

it was

easier to...

I love

spending

time....

The person
I want to
share this
with is...

Thank you for purchasing this book!

I'd love to connect with you and give you a few freebies that
I've created just for my readers!

You can find me here:

www.jenniferrawls.com
Just stop in and say "hello"
Sign up for my monthly newsletter
Find out what I'm writing next
Grab a little something free from me

FACEBOOK
Join my group of Strong Women (and men)!
Take part in the discussions
Be a part of the community

PINTEREST
Check out what inspires me to write upcoming books
Share what's important to you
Get some inspiration to be the Strong Woman you are!

INSTAGRAM
Get inspired
Share a laugh
Let's learn more about each other!

Made in the USA
Monee, IL
25 April 2021